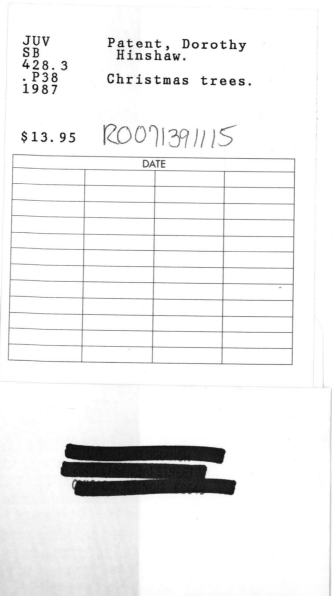

# CHRISTMAS TREES

# CHRISTMAS TREES

Dorothy Hinshaw Patent

Photographs by William Muñoz

DODD, MEAD & COMPANY   NEW YORK

# ACKNOWLEDGMENTS

The author and photographer wish to thank Eric and Christopher Bilderback, Bill Proud, Joe Potoczny, R. D. Kirknes, Richard Inmee, Dick Whitaker, Tom Lawrence, and especially the McHenry family and their employees for their cooperation in this project. Special appreciation goes to Kelly and Mac McHenry for their time and information, and to Kelly McHenry for reading the manuscript.

## PHOTOGRAPH CREDITS

The photograph on page 12 is Courtesy of the White House. Photograph on pages 52–53 by Dorothy Hinshaw Patent. All other photographs are by William Muñoz.

Published by Dodd, Mead & Company, Inc.,
71 Fifth Avenue, New York, N.Y. 10003
Printed in Hong Kong by South China Printing Company
Designed by Jean Krulis

1   2   3   4   5   6   7   8   9   10

*R0071391115*

Library of Congress Cataloging-in-Publication Data
Patent, Dorothy Hinshaw.        Christmas trees.
Includes index.
Summary: Discusses the origins of the Christmas tree and
methods of farming Christmas trees.
1. Christmas tree growing—Juvenile literature.   2. Christmas trees—Juvenile literature.   [1. Christmas trees]   I.
Muñoz, William, ill.   II. Title
SB428.3.P38   1987      394.2'68282      87-9287
ISBN 0-396-09056-7

To the McHenrys with thanks.

# CONTENTS

# ONE
## BEAUTIFUL GREENERY

Christmas is coming soon, and the streets sparkle at night with decorations. It's time to pick out a Christmas tree. The lot smells like fresh pine and fir, and it's full of trees—tall ones and short ones, bushy ones and scrawny ones. Some have long dark green needles, others carry short blue-green ones. It may be hard to choose from such variety, but it's always fun. Since evergreen trees are such a part of Christmas, we tend to take them for granted. But have you ever wondered where they all came from and how they got to be Christmas trees? Do

you know how decorating trees came to be associated with this special holiday?

## BECOMING A CHRISTMAS CUSTOM

Before Christianity came to their lands, people in Germany and Scandinavia brought evergreen trees into their homes during the winter. Life seemed at a standstill outdoors, except for the green needles of the forest pines and firs. By taking some of that greenery into their homes, they could feel the spirit of life, despite the apparent deadness around them.

No one knows how this custom became associated with Christianity, although there are many legends. One is that Martin Luther was so impressed by the glory of the star-filled winter sky that he set up an evergreen tree for his children and decorated it with many lighted candles. He wanted to get across the spirit of Christ, lighting up the world at Christmastime.

However it started, the custom of bringing in a tree and decorating it for Christmas spread in Germany during the 1500s. When German settlers came to America, they brought the Christmas tree tradition with them. In Pennsylvania, where many of them lived, decorated holiday trees began to be common in the 1840s. It took longer for the custom to spread in other parts of the country, but the appeal of a brightly decorated tree was irresistible. In 1856, President Franklin Pierce set up the first White House Christmas tree. America had adopted the Christmas tree as its own.

## LIGHTS AND BAUBLES

In Germany, the early Christmas trees were decorated with colorful paper ornaments and a variety of delicious things to eat—fresh apples, cookies, and candies. Stores sold strings of lustrous glass beads, hard shiny candies, and thin sheets of gold leaf for brightening up nuts and apples. Special colored miniature candles were sold to illuminate the branches.

*Glass ornaments are made in a variety of delicate shapes.*

Modern technology made glass ornaments readily available to the German public in 1867, when natural gas allowed a steady, even flame for reliably producing quantities of thin-walled, colorful glass bubbles. In the United States, it was difficult to get these delicate beauties. Then, in 1889, F. W. Woolworth cautiously offered twenty-five dollars worth of ornaments in his Lancaster, Pennsylvania, store. They sold out in two days, and customers kept asking for more. The next year, Woolworth himself went to Germany and ordered over 200,000 ornaments. Germany remained the center for making glass ornaments through 1939, when the Corning Glass Company set up the first Christmas ornament plant in the United States.

*Every year, a beautifully decorated Christmas tree adorns the White House.*

Meanwhile, the custom of lighting candles on Christmas trees sometimes led to tragedy, when the dried-out branches caught fire. Although only one American family in five had a Christmas tree at the time, General Electric brought out the first electric Christmas tree lights in 1901. From then on, a tree could remain safely lighted for hours. The multicolored glow from strings of lights has become a special part of the beauty of Christmas.

## WHERE DO CHRISTMAS TREES COME FROM?

Some Christmas trees grow in the wild before being cut. In states with lots of national forests that belong to the public, a family may go out into the woods after getting a permit and cut down their own tree for the holiday. Finding an evenly shaped tree in the forest is hard, however. When trees grow close together, the branches can shade one another. Shaded branches don't grow as fast as those exposed to the sun, so wild trees are often quite lopsided.

Wild trees can be cared for to make them better Christmas trees. Some people get permission to use public lands for raising Christmas trees, or they have woods on their own property. They choose the best-looking trees to groom for Christmas. Trees next to them are cut down so that there are five or six feet between, giving them plenty of room to grow. Their branches may be trimmed to help them fill out evenly. Then, after a few years, they are cut down and taken to town for sale.

*Wild trees can be thinned so that they grow into attractive Christmas trees.*

*By removing the lower branches, a tall tree can become a usable Christmas tree.*

*Christmas trees can be grown from stumps by removing some of the branches that sprout from it.*

Even very tall trees can be transformed into holiday decorations. A person harvesting wild trees can cut off all the lower branches and use just the very top as a Christmas tree. The stumps of cut trees can produce Christmas trees also. When the tree is cut, the lowest branches are left on the stump. They are then cut back so that new sprouts form. The sprouts will grow up-

*Wild trees are unloaded from a truck.*

*The trimmed branches from the lower trunks and misshapen trees are put on the bough pile.*

*The boughs can be turned into lovely wreaths.*

ward. The grower selects the strongest sprout or two
and cuts off the others so that all the energy from the
roots goes into growing the new little tree.

18

# TWO
## CHRISTMAS TREE FARMING

In earlier times in North America, forests covered much of the land, and wild trees were abundant. Christmas trees were cut from the woods, and no one thought to raise them on farms. As more people moved to cities and forests were cut down to make room for croplands, wild trees became harder and harder to get. In the 1930s, the first tree farms were started. In the 1950s, growing Christmas trees began to become big business, especially in the northeastern states and around the Great Lakes. In 1960, 5 percent of Christmas trees came from farms, but by 1979, 35 percent did. Today, more than half of all Christmas trees sent to market were grown especially for that purpose on farms from California to New York.

Growing Christmas trees takes a lot of patience. After the tiny trees are planted in neat rows, they must be looked after for six to eight years before they are big enough to be cut. During that time, the trees decorate the landscape and provide a place for wild creatures to live.

*Christmas trees stretch to the horizon in northwestern Montana.*

## BABY TREES

The McHenry farm in Montana's Flathead Valley is devoted mainly to growing Christmas trees sold as far away as Texas and Florida. McHenry trees have even decorated cruise ships in the Caribbean Sea, far away from where they grew near the mountains of Glacier National Park. Many Christmas tree growers buy young trees when they are two to four years old from nurseries. But the McHenrys start from the very beginning by collecting seeds from trees on their own farm. When they find a variety of tree that really grows well for

20

*Evergreens carry their seeds inside cones.*

them, the McHenrys let a few trees stand instead of cutting them down as Christmas trees. After about four more years, the big trees begin to produce cones. The cones are collected and then heated so they pop open and release the seeds. The seeds are vacuumed up and stored for later planting.

A Christmas tree begins its life in a field where the seeds have been scattered, called the seed bed, sending up its tiny first shoot surrounded by others just like it. For two or three years, the little trees grow close together in the seed bed. They are carefully watched over, weeded, and watered.

*The McHenry family grows different kinds of seedlings for Christmas trees.*

Then, when they are two or three years old, the soil around them is loosened by a lifting bar drawn through the soil by a tractor, and they are pulled gently from the ground by hand. The strong and healthy young plants are stored in the cold. When planting time comes in six to eight weeks, their roots are trimmed to about eight inches long. That way, when a seedling is planted, its roots won't be bent unnaturally upward but can stretch downward as they grow, producing a strong, healthy root system.

After another year of growing, the seedlings have stout little trunks and healthy, bushy roots. They are

*Kelly McHenry drives the tractor along a seedling bed, loosening them from the soil.*

A bar runs under the roots of the seedlings to loosen them.

Young trees are collected from the ground.

The young trees are sorted by size. Some of them are replanted at Mc-Henry's farm, and some are sold to other growers.

These young trees have strong, healthy roots.

Trimming the roots.

This is the tree planter, lifted up so you can see the plow blade on the bottom. As the planter moves forward, the plow makes a furrow.

While Kelly carefully drives the tractor pulling the tree planter between rows of newly placed trees, other people plant more trees in the ground.

Each person has a box of young trees to plant.

The young tree is placed in a holder on the planter. As the planter moves forward, the tree is carried to the ground, where it is placed in the furrow made by the plow.

As the trees are planted, the wheels close up the furrow and press the earth alongside the trees.

Two of the first four rows planted in the field. The other two rows can be seen in the upper right of the picture. The space between the two sets of rows is where the tractor drove.

*These tiny seedlings will grow up to be fine, tall Christmas trees.*

ready to be transplanted one last time, into the field where they will become shapely, handsome trees. The field is smoothed out to receive the new crop, and the little trees are planted six feet apart in both directions, giving them plenty of room to grow.

## CARING FOR THE TREES

Trees take little from the soil, so they can be grown on land that won't produce other, more demanding crops. Rich soil is actually not good for Christmas trees because they can grow too fast. The tip of the trunk, called the leader, grows more quickly in fertile ground. Each year in the spring, the leader puts out a new set of branches, called a whorl. If the tree grows too fast, the whorls can be far apart, making the tree scrawny and unappealing. A tree that grows more slowly will be bushier, with its whorls closer together. For this reason, most tree farmers do not fertilize their trees. Because

*These spruce are growing into nice, bushy trees. Each has a leader growing straight up, where no branches have formed yet.*

their roots grow deeply into the earth, the trees do not need to be watered either, once they are set out into the field. The rain provided by nature gives them enough moisture.

Even though the farmer doesn't need to water or fertilize his crop, he still must take good care of it. Weeds can grow between the trees, competing with them for sunlight and moisture. To keep the weeds under control, the McHenrys sometimes spray chemicals, called herbicides, that kill growing plants. The herbicides are used in the early spring or in the fall while the trees are not growing. Since only the weeds take in the herbicide and are killed, the Christmas crop is unharmed.

The trees can also be attacked by a variety of insect

*Herbicides aren't the only way to control weeds. Another way of keeping weeds down is to cultivate the ground between rows of trees. Blades on the back of the tractor turn over the soil, exposing the roots of any weeds and killing them.*

*This little tree is misshapen from deer feeding on it.*

pests and diseases. When one of these threatens, the trees are sprayed with chemicals to kill the invaders. Deer present a different problem. When their natural food is in short supply during the winter, deer raid the farm, munching on the branches of the trees and destroying their lovely, even shapes.

Winter can bring other problems, too. If there is snow on the ground and the weather is sunny, the sunlight is reflected off the white snow onto the tree. This intense light can actually kill the needles along the south side of the tree where the sun hits the branches if there are many sunny days. For this reason, the best areas for

31

*Sunlight reflecting off the snow killed branches on the south side of this tree.*

*Each of these Christmas trees ready to ship has a good handle on the bottom.*

32

growing Christmas trees in the north are those with cloudy winters.

## BECOMING A CHRISTMAS TREE

After they are transplanted, the young trees are left to grow on their own for two years. Then, the first steps in turning the strong young plants into Christmas trees begin. A Christmas tree needs a "handle" at the bottom so it can be easily picked up and so that it can be placed in a holder when it graces a home for the holidays. After

the trees have been out in the field for two years, all branches below the first even whorl of strong branches are cut off, and any needles growing on the trunk are rubbed away. This leaves a nice clean handle eight to twelve inches long for carrying the tree and setting it up.

Everyone wants a shapely Christmas tree with lots of branches. To get that way, a tree may need help. Pines, spruces, and firs are all grown on tree farms, but fast-growing pines are the most popular. In a warm sunny summer with good rainfall, a pine tree can grow as much as thirty inches in height. Even when growing at a slow, even pace, pine trees are likely to grow too quickly to produce nice, bushy trees on their own. After resting through the cold winter, a pine tree wakes up in the warm spring weather and begins to grow. A new whorl branches off, and the leader quickly lengthens. If the tree is left alone, the branches and leader will continue to grow until midsummer. Then, the buds for next year's whorl will form as summer turns into fall.

When pines are about two feet tall, this natural growth process is interrupted for the first time. The trees are "sheared"—trimmed by clippers or a knife—to control their growth and help them develop a nice, even shape. The branches and leader are cut back in late June or in July, near the end of the growing season. This stops their growth for the year. The leader is cut back to about a foot, and a new set of buds forms just below the cut. The following spring, the bud closest to the cut forms a new leader, and the rest grow a new whorl.

*This little tree has been sheared for the first time.*

*The branches are sheared by a quick slice of the shearing knife.*

*Trimming the leader.*

Spruce trees need little or no shearing, since they grow more slowly than pines and naturally form a more bushy tree. If they do need some trimming, it can be done after the trees have stopped growing. Unlike pines, spruce and fir produce extra branches and buds along the leader as a natural part of their growth. If the tree is cut back after growth has stopped, these buds will grow the next season to make a new leader and whorls.

*The leader after trimming.*   *New buds grow just below the cut end of the leader.*

*Spruce trees grow extra branches along the trunks during the year.*

# THREE
# CHRISTMAS IS COMING!

For many long years, the Christmas tree farmer tends his trees, protecting them from hungry insects and diseases, keeping down the weeds so they can grow, and shearing them to make them into lovely holiday decorations. Six or more years after transplanting, the trees are finally tall enough to be cut.

Preparations for Christmas can begin as early as August on a Christmas tree farm. Some varieties of pine tend to turn yellow in the fall, and no one wants a yellow Christmas tree. Such trees are sprayed with a tree-green paint in August. The trees don't look painted at all, but stay the same rich green color they had in August even at the end of December.

At McHenrys', workers go through the fields of seven-year-old trees in the fall, marking each one over six feet, three inches in height with a plastic tag at the top. The weather controls when cutting begins, for it tells the trees when to begin resting for the winter. You might think that a tree cut as close to Christmas as possible

*These shapely Scotch pines are ready to harvest.*

*The trees with tags will be cut, while the others will be left to grow for another year.*

would last the longest, but this isn't necessarily so. The tree must be in just the right resting stage for it to survive cutting and standing in a warm house without dropping its needles.

## Harvest Time

The McHenry family watch the wild larch trees to time their harvest. When the larch turn yellow, their plantation trees are ready to be cut. The trees will have set their needles so they won't fall off easily, but they

*When the larch turn yellow in northwestern Montana, it's time to harvest the Christmas trees.*

will still have some vital sap in the branches. If the trees are cut too late, after the really cold weather begins, the trees will have sent too much sap into the roots, and the branches will be brittle. Because they are in a deep stage of rest then, they will not look as fresh and alive. If such trees are cut and brought into a warm house, they are likely to lose their needles quickly. At high altitudes, wild trees may be cut as early as September, for winter comes early in the mountains.

Usually, the harvest of plantation trees takes place in October. The McHenrys use a special tree cutting machine to make the work go quickly. They harvest the seven-year-old pines that are tall enough and all the pines left in the eight-year-old fields.

*The trees are cut.*

Cut Scotch pines in the field.

The old needles on the inside of the tree are dead.

*The butt of the tree is placed in a slot on the shaker.*

*The bar holding the slots vibrates fast, shaking the needles from the trees.*

After being cut, pines must be vigorously shaken to get rid of the old needles that lodge among the branches. Pines usually keep their needles for only two years and shed all three-year-old needles. Some of the needles fall to the ground, but more get stuck in the tree. Shaking the trees is a hard job that takes a crew of five people. They can shake up to two thousand trees in a day.

## PREPARING TO SHIP

A Christmas tree is three or four feet in diameter and takes up a lot of space. Most trees are shipped by truck to where they are sold, and the more trees that fit on a truck, the less expensive shipping will be. The trees are made smaller by baling them—using twine or

*The dead needles shake out of the tree.*

plastic netting to hold the branches against the trunk. Baling also protects the branches from breaking during shipping and handling.

The McHenrys use a string baling machine. Each tree is fed stump first into a funnel, which gently presses the branches towards the top. As the tree moves through the funnel, twine is wrapped around the branches. When the tree is baled, it is lined up with colored markers to determine its size. Then it is tagged so that it will be easy to sort the trees by size later on.

The string baler can make a big difference in ship-

*While the tree passes through the cone in the center of the baler, the twine holder (with the green label) spins around it, wrapping it with twine.*

*A pine is loaded into the baler.*

ping. After baling, the trees are less than a foot-and-a-half in diameter, and about a thousand of them will fit on one semitruck load. Loading the trees on the truck is tricky. They are laid carefully in layers in such a way that a person walking on them to load or unload steps only on the butts. That way, none of the branches will be broken.

47

*It comes out the other end onto the metal table with color markings for different sized trees.*

*The tree is tagged to show its size.*

*The baled trees are piled waiting for pickup.*

# FOUR
## YOUR OWN CHRISTMAS TREE

After years of being carefully raised and groomed to be Christmas trees, this year's crop is on the lots, waiting to be bought by families to brighten their holidays. If you take some time choosing your tree, you can enjoy it more than if you just grab the first one that will fit into your house.

## WHAT KIND OF TREE?

Many kinds of trees are grown for Christmas. There are pines, spruces, and firs of several kinds, each with its own special traits. In different parts of the country, trees unique to that area are grown.

Pines have long needles that appear in bundles of two to five. Norway pine is sold in some parts of the country. Its needles are very long—about three inches—so it is difficult to decorate. Scotch pine is the most common tree raised on farms. It grows quickly and takes on a lovely shape when sheared. Scotch pine needles are about an inch-and-a-half long. There are many varieties of Scotch pine, some with dark green needles, others with blue-green or yellowish needles. The biggest

*How do you pick which kind of tree to buy?*

*Monterey pines grow on a farm in California's Ojai Valley.*

Pine trees, like this wild, naturally flocked ponderosa, have long needles. The flocked look is caused by ice crystals deposited on the needles by fog.

Christmas trees can be sprayed with plastic foam to look like naturally flocked trees.

54

advantage of buying a pine for Christmas is that it will last a long time in a warm house without losing its needles.

Spruce trees have short needles, less than an inch long. They are stiff and pointed and feel sharp. Since spruce have strong branches, they can bear heavy decorations. The Norway spruce has dark green needles and a nice shape. Spruces shouldn't be bought weeks before Christmas, for they lose their needles quickly in a warm room.

*Spruce trees come in a variety of shades of green. Notice the pine, with its longer needles, in the center.*

Fir trees are especially popular for Christmas. Their needles are longer than spruce, but not so stiff and sharp. Firs have nice shapes, and their strong branches will carry decorations well. The balsam fir, with its delightful fresh aroma, has always been a Christmas favorite. If fresh, this tree will hold its needles well in a dry room. But if it was cut weeks before and shipped, it can drop them quite quickly.

The Douglas fir, sometimes sold as Montana fir, is actually a pine, but it looks more like a fir. In recent years, this lovely tree has increased in popularity. Wild

*This family has chosen a Douglas fir to decorate their home.*

*Opposite: This tall alpine fir will make a spectacular Christmas tree.*

Douglas firs are cut, and they are also grown on farms. The problem for growers in the north is that it takes up to ten years to grow a Douglas fir tall enough for the market. But its pleasing shape and its ability to hold onto its inch-long needles in a warm, dry room have made growing this tree worth the time.

## CHOOSING THE TREE

The most expensive trees bear their branches evenly all around. But if you put your tree in a corner, a cheaper, lopsided tree would be perfectly fine. Feel the needles of the tree. If they are flexible and a healthy green color, the tree is probably quite fresh. If the needles show brown or fall off, the tree is too old.

When you set up your tree at home, either use a sturdy holder that will contain water or set the tree in a bucket, fill with sand, and add water. Even though the tree is cut, it is in some ways still alive and can take up water to retain its freshness. Before setting it up, check the cut end of the tree. When a tree is harvested, the trunk leaks resin over the cut end. This helps hold in moisture and keeps the tree fresh. But when it is brought into a warm house, the tree needs more water. At the lot, the trunk should have been recut so that the channels that carry water into the tree are not clogged. If the cut end of the trunk is sticky and covered with resin, saw off about an inch so that the tree can take in water.

Christmas trees are fun, but they can also cause

problems. If you have a dog, putting the tree in a corner will help keep it from being knocked over. To keep it from drying out, locate it away from direct sunlight and heat ducts or radiators. When the family leaves the house, the lights on the tree should be turned off to protect from fire.

Once your tree is carefully located and provided with water, you can decorate it with your favorite lights and ornaments, knowing that it will last through the holidays, bringing the freshness of the outdoors into your home. All you have to do now is put the presents under the tree and wait until Christmas!

*Presents under the tree until Christmas.*

# INDEX

## ABOUT THE AUTHOR

DOROTHY HINSHAW PATENT was born in Minnesota and spent most of her growing-up years in Marin County, California. She has a Ph.D. in zoology from the University of California at Berkeley.

Dr. Patent is the author of more than twenty-five nonfiction books for children of various ages, from preschool through high school, including *Baby Horses, The Sheep Book, Maggie, A Sheep Dog,* and *Wheat: The Golden Harvest.*

She lives in Missoula, Montana, with her husband and two sons.

## ABOUT THE PHOTOGRAPHER

WILLIAM MUÑOZ lives in St. Ignatius, Montana, with his wife, Sandy, on a farm where they raise horses and cattle.

He studied at the University of Montana where he earned a BA in history. Bill Muñoz has been a photographer for over eighteen years and has collaborated with Dorothy Hinshaw Patent on many of her children's books.